1948 U.S.

YEARBOOK

ISBN: 9781790460236

INDEX

FIRST EDITION

PEOPLE IN HIGH OFFICE

Harry S. Truman
April 12, 1945 - January 20, 1953
Democratic Party

Born May 8, 1884, Truman served as the 33rd President of the United States succeeding to the presidency on April 12, 1945 when Roosevelt died after months of declining health. Harry S. Truman died December 26, 1972.

48 stars (1912-1959)

Vice President: *(Vacant 1945-1949)*
Chief Justice: Fred M. Vinson
Speaker of the House of Representatives: Joseph William Martin, Jr.
Senate Majority Leader: Wallace H. White, Jr.

UNITED KINGDOM

Monarch **King George VI**	**Prime Minister** **Clement Attlee**

Dec 11, 1936 - Feb 6, 1952	Jul 26, 1945 - Oct 26, 1951

Australia	**Canada**	**Ireland**

Prime Minister **Ben Chifley** Labor Party July 13, '45 - Dec 19, '49	Prime Minister **Mackenzie King** Liberal Party Oct 23, '35 - Nov 15, '48	Taoiseach of Ireland **John A. Costello** Fine Gael Feb 18, '48 - Jun 13, '51

	Brazil	**President** Eurico Gaspar Dutra (1946-1951)
	China	**Premiers** Zhang Qun (1947-1948) Weng Wenhao (1948) Sun Fo (1948-1949)
	Cuba	**Presidents** Ramón Grau (1944-1948) Carlos Prío Socarrás (1948-1952)
	France	**President** Vincent Auriol (1947-1954)
	Germany	**Under Allied Military Occupation** by Britain, France, U.S. & Soviet Union
	India	**Prime Minister** Jawaharlal Nehru (1947-1964)
	Italy	**Prime Minister** Alcide De Gasperi (1945-1953)

Japan

Prime Ministers
Tetsu Katayama (1947-1948)
Hitoshi Ashida (1948)
Shigeru Yoshida (1948-1954)

Mexico

President
Miguel Alemán Valdés (1946-1952)

New Zealand

Prime Minister
Peter Fraser (1940-1949)

Pakistan

Prime Minister
Liaquat Ali Khan (1947-1951)

Spain

President
Francisco Franco (1938-1973)

South Africa

Prime Ministers
Jan Smuts (1939-1948)
Daniel François Malan (1948-1954)

Soviet Union

Communist Party Leader
Joseph Stalin (1922-1953)

Turkey

Prime Minister
Hasan Saka (1947-1949)

EVENTS FROM 1948

JANUARY

1	The New Jersey State Constitution of 1947 goes into effect.
10	'Call Me Mister' closes at National Theatre, NYC after 734 performances. In 1951 20th Century Fox release a film version starring Betty Grable.
29	A Douglas DC-3 plane crashes at Los Gatos Creek, California killing 4 U.S. citizens and 28 deportees. The incident inspires the much covered song 'Deportee' by Woody Guthrie.
30	The inventor and pioneer aviator Orville Wright (born August 19, 1871) dies of a heart attack.
30 - Feb 8	The 5th Winter Olympic games open in St Moritz, Switzerland. 28 nations and 669 athletes compete in 22 events over 4 different sports during the 10 days of the games. The U.S. team take home 3 gold, 4 silver and 2 bronze medals.

Orville Wright at the controls of the 'Wright Flyer' as his brother Wilbur Wright looks on during the plane's first flight four miles south of Kitty Hawk, North Carolina.

The Wright brothers are generally credited with inventing, building and flying the world's first successful airplane. They made the first controlled, sustained flight of a powered, heavier-than-air aircraft on December 17, 1903. In 1904-05 the brothers developed their flying machine into the first practical fixed-wing aircraft. Although not the first to build and fly experimental aircraft, the Wright brothers were the first to invent aircraft controls that made fixed-wing powered flight possible.

8

3   Eighteen-year-old Dick Button becomes first Olympic figure skating champion from U.S. Button led the field after the compulsory skate and then won the gold medal by becoming the first person to ever complete a double axel in competition. His success would continue beyond the games winning the gold medal at the 1952 Olympics as well as 5 World Championship gold medals between 1948 and 1952.

7   Omar Bradley succeeds Dwight Eisenhower as Army Chief of Staff. During WW2 Bradley commanded all U.S. ground forces invading Germany from the west. This included forty-three divisions and 1.3 million men, the largest body of American soldiers ever to serve under a single U.S. field commander. Bradley was the last of only nine people to hold a five-star rank in the U.S. Armed Forces.

21   NASCAR, founded by Bill France Sr., is incorporated.

1948 NASCAR Modified Championship winner Red Byron with his mechanic Red Vogt.

The first sanctioned NASCAR (National Association for Stock Car Auto Racing) race was held on Daytona's beach course and was won by Red Byron in his Ford Modified. Byron went on to become NASCAR's first Modified champion in 1948 and its first Strictly Stock (predecessor to Sprint Cup) champion in 1949. NASCAR is now motorsport's preeminent stock-car racing organization and sanctions over 1,500 races at over 100 tracks in 39 of the 50 U.S. states as well as in Canada.

MARCH

8   The United States Supreme Court rules, in the case of McCollum v. Board of Education, that religious instruction in public schools violates the U.S. Constitution.

MARCH

10   Herb H. Hoover becomes the first civilian to exceed speed of sound (and only the second person ever to do so) in a NACA XS-1 (Bell X-1) rocket research aircraft.

16   Billie Holiday is released from prison early due to good behaviour. She had been arrested on May 16, 1947 for possession of narcotics at her New York apartment.

17   The Hells Angels Motorcycle Club is founded in California.

20   Renowned Italian conductor Arturo Toscanini makes his television debut conducting the NBC Symphony Orchestra in an all-Wagner program.

25   Meteorologists at Tinker Air Force Base in Oklahoma City issue the world's first tornado forecast which is verified when a tornado strikes the base that evening.

Headliner Billie Holiday on stage Carnegie Hall, New York City.

March 27: Billie Holiday (born Eleanora Fagan, April 7, 1915 - July 17, 1959), plays Carnegie Hall just 11 days after her release from prison. All 2,700 tickets are sold in advance (a record at the time for the venue). Holiday was so nervous backstage that she pricked herself while pinning a gardenia in her hair. The performance was a triumphant comeback.

APRIL

3   President Harry Truman signs the Marshall Plan (officially the European Recovery Program, ERP). The initiative was to aid Western Europe by giving over $5 billion (approximately $50 billion today) in economic support to help rebuild Western European economies after the end of World War II.

APRIL

3 Ludwig van Beethoven's Ninth Symphony is played on television in its entirety for the first time in a concert featuring Arturo Toscanini conducting the NBC Symphony Orchestra. The chorus is conducted by Robert Shaw.

19 The American Broadcasting Company (ABC) TV network debuts. Its first ever broadcast, On the Corner, features satirist Henry Morgan. ABC originally launched on October 12, 1943 as a radio network.

20 New York City hikes its subway fare from 5 cents to 10 cents. The bus fare increases to 7 cents.

30 The Charter of the Organization of the American States, a Pan-American treaty that sets out the creation of the Organization of American States, is signed by 21 countries in Bogotá, Colombia. The treaty came into effect on December 13, 1951.

MAY

1 Idaho Senator Glenn Taylor is arrested in Birmingham, Alabama for attempting to use a door reserved for African Americans rather than the whites-only door. He was attempting to attend a meeting of the Southern Negro Youth Congress and was subsequently convicted of disorderly conduct.

3 The Pulitzer Prize for Drama is awarded to Tennessee Williams for 'A Streetcar Named Desire'. The play opened on Broadway on December 3, 1947 and starred Jessica Tandy, Marlon Brando, Karl Malden and Kim Hunter. A Streetcar Named Desire is often regarded as among the finest plays of the 20th century.

14 The United States recognizes the new state of Israel.

19 The Mundt-Nixon Bill of 1948 fails to pass U.S. Senate. The bill proposed that all members of the Communist Party of the United States would be required register with the Attorney General.

21 New York Yankee Joe DiMaggio completes the cycle (hitting a single, double, triple and home run in the same game).

26 The U.S. Congress passes Public Law 557 which permanently establishes the Civil Air Patrol as an auxiliary of the United States Air Force.

30 A dike along the Columbia River breaks obliterating Vanport, Oregon within minutes. 15 people die and tens of thousands are left homeless.

JUNE

3 The Palomar Observatory 200-inch Hale telescope is finished in California. The telescope sees first light on January 26, 1949 targeting NGC 2261. It was built by Caltech with a $6 million grant from the Rockefeller Foundation and was the largest telescope in the world for 45 years.

8 Edith Kermit Carow Roosevelt (born August 6, 1861) dies. She was the second wife of President Theodore Roosevelt and served as First Lady of the United States during his presidency from 1901 to 1909.

8 John E. Rudder becomes the first black Marine officer commissioned in the regular United States Marine Corps.

11 The first ever primate astronaut Albert, a rhesus monkey, is launched into space from White Sands, New Mexico by the U.S. He rode over 39 miles on a V-2 rocket but died of suffocation during the flight. Albert was followed by Albert II who managed to survive the V-2 flight but unfortunately died on impact on June 14, 1949 after a parachute failure.

12   The United States Congress passed the Women's Armed Services Integration Act enabling women to serve as permanent, regular members of the armed forces (in the Army, Navy, Marine Corps and the recently formed Air Force). Prior to this act women, with the exception of nurses, served in the military only in times of war.

17   United Air Lines Flight 624, a Douglas DC-6 four-engine propeller-driven airplane, crashes at 1:41pm Eastern Daylight Time outside of Aristes, Pennsylvania. All 4 crew members and 39 passengers on board are killed.

25   Joe Louis KO's Jersey Joe Walcott in 11 rounds to retain The Ring and world heavyweight titles at the Yankee Stadium in New York City.

26   The U.S. begins airlift Operation Vittles to West Berlin in response to the Berlin Blockade.

28   David Lean's Oliver Twist, based on Charles Dickens's famous novel, premieres in the UK. It is banned for 3 years in the U.S. because of alleged anti-Semitism in depicting master criminal Fagin who was played by Alec Guinness.

Young Berliners watch a Douglas C-54 Skymaster landing at Tempelhof Airport.

The Berlin Blockade was one of the first major international crises of the Cold War. During the multinational occupation of post–World War II Germany, the Soviet Union blocked the Western Allies' railway, road and canal access to the sectors of Berlin under Western control. In response, the Allies organized the Berlin airlift to carry supplies to the people of West Berlin. Aircrews from the United States, Britain, Canada, Australia, New Zealand and South Africa flew over 200,000 flights in one year, providing to the West Berliners up to 8,893 tons of necessities each day. By the spring of 1949 the airlift was clearly succeeding and by April it was delivering more cargo than had previously been transported into the city by rail. On May 12, 1949 the USSR lifted the blockade of West Berlin.

JULY

20 President Harry S. Truman issues the second peacetime military draft in the United States amid increasing tensions with the Soviet Union (the first peacetime draft occurred in 1940 under President Roosevelt).

26 President Truman signs Executive Order 9981 abolishing racial discrimination in the United States Armed Forces. This eventually leads to the end of segregation in the services.

26 Bob Howard becomes the first black host of a network television show on CBS's Bob Howard Show.

31 New York International Airport is dedicated at Idlewild Field in New York City. It is renamed John F. Kennedy International Airport in 1963 after President Kennedy's assassination.

31 Soviet spy Elizabeth Bentley testifies before The House Un-American Activities Committee (HUAC).

AUGUST

1 The U.S. Air Force Office of Special Investigations is founded.

10 Allen Funt's Candid Camera makes its TV debut on ABC.

16 Baseball player Babe Ruth (born February 6, 1895) dies of cancer aged 53. Instead of a wake at a funeral home his casket is taken to Yankee Stadium where it remains for two days. 77,000 people file past to pay tribute to him. His funeral Mass took place at St. Patrick's Cathedral with a crowd estimated at 75,000 waiting outside.

27 The temperature reaches 102°F in Cleveland - the highest ever recorded for August.

SEPTEMBER

September 27: Laurence Olivier's movie Hamlet premieres in Los Angeles, California and becomes the first British film to win the Academy Award for Best Picture. Olivier himself also wins the Academy Award for Best Actor in this film.

OCTOBER

11 The Cleveland Indians defeat the Boston Braves to win the World Series 4 games to 2.

OCTOBER

16 The 57th Street Art Fair, the oldest juried art fair in the American Midwest, is founded by Mary Louise Womer, the proprietor of The Little Gallery on 57th Street.

27 - 31 A wall of smog kills 20 people and sickens 7,000 more in Donora, Pennsylvania.

NOVEMBER

2 Incumbent President Harry S. Truman, the Democratic nominee who had succeeded to the presidency after the death of President Franklin D. Roosevelt in 1945, successfully runs for election against Republican nominee Thomas E. Dewey.

26 The first polaroid camera sells in Boston, Massachusetts.

30 Baseball's second Negro National League (established in 1933) disbands.

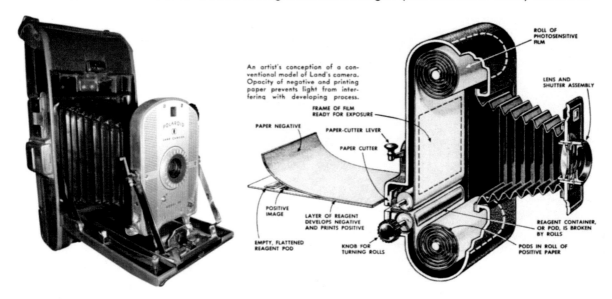

An artist's conception of a conventional model of Land's camera. Opacity of negative and printing paper prevents light from interfering with developing process.

The first polaroid camera sells for $89.75 at the Jordan Marsh department store in Boston, Massachusetts. The Land Camera model 95 makes more than $5 million in sales in its first year and becomes the prototype for all Polaroid Land Cameras produced for the next 15 years.

DECEMBER

American-born British poet T.S. Eliot wins the Nobel Prize in Literature for 'his outstanding pioneer contribution to present-day poetry'.

2 St. Louis Cardinals Stan Musial is picked as the National League's MVP for the third time (1943, 1946 and 1948)..

8 American football's 14th Heisman Trophy Award is awarded to Southern Methodist University's Doak Walker. Walker went on to play professionally in the NFL with the Detroit Lions for six seasons.

15 The United States Department of Justice formally charges Alger Hiss on two counts of perjury.

28 The Douglas DST airliner NC16002 disappears 50 miles south of Miami, Florida carrying 29 passengers and 3 crew. No probable cause for the loss was ever determined by the official investigation and its disappearance remains unsolved.

UNDATED U.S. EVENTS FROM 1948

- The Fresh Kills Landfill expansion is approved on Staten Island, New York making it the world's largest landfill site.
- The first of the Kinsey Reports, Sexual Behavior in the Human Male, is published.
- Charles Lazarus founds Children's Supermart (the predecessor of Toys R Us) in Washington, D.C. as a baby-furniture retailer.
- The Wright Flyer goes on display in the Smithsonian.
- The first commercially available cat litter, Kitty Litter, went on sale. It was invented by Ed Lowe and was so successful that by the time of Lowe's death his company was worth half a billion dollars.
- John and Margaret Walson create the first cable television company (Service Electric Cable Television) in the mountains of Pennsylvania.

OTHER NOTEABLE WORLDWIDE EVENTS

1. January 30 - Mahatma Gandhi is assassinated in New Delhi by Hindu militant Nathuram Godse. Godse and his co-conspirator were tried and executed in 1949.
2. April 7 - The World Health Organization (WHO) is established by the United Nations and is headquartered in Geneva, Switzerland. The WHO Constitution states that its objective is 'the attainment by all people of the highest possible level of health'.
3. Georges de Mestral, an engineer from Switzerland, first starts his work on inventing hook and loop fasteners. By 1955 he had successfully patented his idea and named his invention Velcro (formed from the two French words: velours for velvet and crochet for hook).
4. June 18 - Columbia Records unveil the LP record at a New York press conference. Developed by Peter Goldmark of CBS Laboratories the LP is a 12-inch (30 cm) Long Play (LP) 33 1/3 rpm microgroove record album. 1949 sees RCA Victor follow this with the first 45 rpm single which measures 7 inches in diameter.
5. Bertram Forer demonstrates the Forer effect in that people tend to accept generalised descriptions of personality as uniquely applicable to themselves.
6. The Manchester Small-Scale Experimental Machine, the world's first stored-program computer, runs its first program. Nicknamed Baby it was built at the Victoria University of Manchester, England by Frederic C. Williams, Tom Kilburn and Geoff Tootill.
7. The 1948 Summer Olympics, officially known as the Games of the XIV Olympiad, were held in London, England. After a 12-year hiatus because of World War II, these were the first Olympics since the 1936 Games in Berlin. Germany and Japan were refused permission to participate and although the USSR was invited it chose not to send any athletes.
8. 20-year-old Newman Darby invents windsurfing. In 1948 he was the first to conceive the idea of using a handheld sail and rig mounted on a universal joint so that he could control his small catamaran - the first rudderless sailboard ever built that allowed a person to steer by shifting his or her weight in order to tilt the sail fore and aft.
9. November 20 - The Takahē, a flightless bird generally thought to have been extinct for fifty years, is rediscovered by Geoffrey Orbell near Lake Te Anau on the South Island of New Zealand.
10. December 10 - The Universal Declaration of Human Rights (UDHR) is adopted by the United Nations General Assembly at the Palais de Chaillot in Paris.

U.S. PERSONALITIES

BORN IN 1948

Carl Weathers
January 14, 1948

Actor and former professional football player who is best known for playing Apollo Creed in the Rocky series of films. Other prominent film roles have included Predator (1987), Happy Gilmore (1996) and Little Nicky (2000). Weathers' brief professional football career included seven games in 1970 and one in 1971 for the Oakland Raiders and 10 games for the BC Lions of the Canadian Football League between 1971 and 1973.

Anita Marie Pointer
January 23, 1948

R&B/Soul singer-songwriter best known as a founding member of the Grammy Award winning vocal group The Pointer Sisters. She and her sisters found fame in 1973 when 'Yes We Can Can' reached No.11 on the Billboard Hot 100. In 1974 Anita's writing talents helped the group make music history when 'Fairytale' became a hit on the country music charts enabling The Pointer Sisters to become the first black female group to perform at the Grand Ole Opry.

Alice Cooper - Vincent Damon Furnier
February 4, 1948

Singer, songwriter and actor whose career spans over five decades. With his distinctive raspy voice and a stage show that features guillotines, electric chairs, fake blood, deadly snakes, baby dolls and dueling swords, Cooper is considered by music journalists and peers alike to be 'The Godfather of Shock Rock'. His hits include 'School's Out' and 'Eighteen' and he was inducted into the Rock and Roll Hall of Fame in 2011.

Teller - Raymond Joseph Teller
February 14, 1948

Magician, illusionist, actor, comedian, writer, director and half of the comedy magic duo Penn & Teller (along with Penn Jillette). He is an atheist, debunker, skeptic and a fellow of the Cato Institute, an organization which is featured prominently in the duo's Showtime television series Bullshit! (2003-2010). In 2013 Penn & Teller were honored with a star on the Hollywood Walk of Fame and with the Magicians Of The Year Award from the Magic Castle.

Ronald Charles Cey
February 15, 1948

Former professional baseball player who played for the Los Angeles Dodgers (1971-1982), Chicago Cubs (1983-1986) and Oakland Athletics (1987). During his career he was known by the nickname The Penguin, a name which had been given to him by his college coach. Cey was a six-time All Star (1974-1979) and played in the 1981 World Series, helping the Dodgers to four straight victories after losing their first two games. He was named co-MVP along with Steve Yeager and Pedro Guerrero.

Bernadette Peters
February 28, 1948

Actress, singer and children's book author whose career has spanned five decades. She has starred in musical theatre, films and television, as well as performing in solo concerts and recordings. Peters is one of the most critically acclaimed Broadway performers having received nominations for seven Tony Awards, winning two (plus an honorary award), and nine Drama Desk Awards, winning three. She received a star on the Hollywood Walk of Fame in 1987.

James Vernon Taylor
March 12, 1948

Singer-songwriter and guitarist. Taylor achieved his breakthrough in 1970 with the No.3 single Fire And Rain and had his first No.1 hit the following year with You've Got A Friend. His 1976 Greatest Hits album was certified Diamond, selling over 12 million copies, and every other album that he released from 1977 to 2007 sold over a million copies. A five-time Grammy Award winner he was inducted into the Rock and Roll Hall of Fame in 2000.

William Edward 'Billy' Crystal
March 14, 1948

Actor, writer, producer, director, comedian and television host. He gained prominence in the 1970s for playing Jodie Dallas on the ABC sitcom Soap, and became a Hollywood film star after appearing in the critical box office successes When Harry Met Sally (1989), City Slickers (1991) and Analyze This (1999). He also provided the voice of Mike Wazowski in the Monsters, Inc. franchise and has hosted the Academy Awards on 9 occasions from 1990 to 2012.

Steven Tyler - Steven Victor Tallarico
March 26, 1948

Singer-songwriter, multi-instrumentalist and former television music competition judge, who best known as the lead singer of the Boston-based rock band Aerosmith. He was ranked third on Hit Parader's Top 100 Metal Vocalists of All Time and in 2001 was inducted into the Rock and Roll Hall of Fame with Aerosmith. In 2013 Tyler and his song writing partner Joe Perry received the ASCAP Founders Award and were inducted into the Songwriters Hall of Fame.

Rhea Jo Perlman
March 31, 1948

Actress who is best known for playing the feisty barmaid Carla from the television show Cheers (for which she won four Emmy Awards). She began her acting career in 1972 when she played a bit role in the film Hot Dogs For Gauguin. That same year she appeared in Up - An Uppity Revue alongside her future husband Danny DeVito. Since 2014 she has starred in a recurring role on The Mindy Project as Danny's mother Annette Castellano.

Albert Arnold 'Al' Gore Jr.
March 31, 1948

Politician and environmentalist who served as the 45th Vice President of the United States from 1993 to 2001 under President Bill Clinton. After leaving office he remained prominent as an author and environmental activist whose work in climate change activism earned him (jointly with the IPCC) the Nobel Peace Prize in 2007. In 2009 Gore also won a Grammy Award for Best Spoken Word Album for his book An Inconvenient Truth.

**Silas Merritt 'Si'
Robertson**
April 27, 1948

Television personality, preacher, hunter, outdoorsman and retired U.S. Army soldier who is best known for his role on A&E's Duck Dynasty (a reality television series that portrays the lives of the Robertson family and their family operated business). He has also appeared on other shows such as the Outdoor Channel's Buck Commander and The Duckmen of Louisiana, and was the eponymous host of the Duck Dynasty spin-off Going Si-Ral.

**Stephanie Lynn
'Stevie' Nicks**
May 26, 1948

Multi-award winning singer-songwriter who is often regarded as the Queen of Rock n' Roll. Nicks is best known for both her work as the front woman of Fleetwood Mac and for her extensive, multi-platinum solo career. Collectively these have produced over 40 top-50 hits and sold over 140 million records making her one of the best-selling music acts of all time. She was inducted into the Rock and Roll Hall of Fame in 1998.

Phylicia Rashad
June 19, 1948

Actress, singer and stage director who is best known for her role as Clair Huxtable on the long-running NBC sitcom The Cosby Show (1984-1992). In 2004, she became the first black actress to win the Tony Award for Best Actress in a Play, which she won for her role in the revival of A Raisin In The Sun. Rashad has also appeared in a number of films including For Colored Girls (2010), Steel Magnolias (2012) and Creed (2015).

**Kathleen Doyle
'Kathy' Bates**
June 28, 1948

Actress who began her career on the stage and was nominated for the Tony Award for Best Lead Actress in a Play in 1983 for her performance in 'night, Mother. Bates rose to prominence with her performance in Misery (1990) for which she won the Academy Award and Golden Globe for Best Actress. In total, for her television work, she has received fourteen Emmy Award nominations - winning two for her roles in both Harry's Law and American Horror Story: Coven.

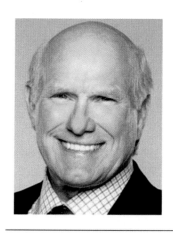

Terry Paxton Bradshaw
September 2, 1948

Legendary Pittsburgh Steelers quarterback who led the team to 4 Super Bowl Championships in a six-year period (1974, 1975, 1978 and 1979). He was selected first overall by The Steelers in the 1970 NFL Draft and led them to eight AFC Central championships. He was inducted into the Pro Football Hall of Fame in 1989 in his first year of eligibility and since 1994 has been working as a TV analyst and co-host of Fox NFL Sunday.

Nathaniel 'Tiny' Archibald
September 2, 1948

Retired professional basketball player who spent 14 years playing in the NBA (1970-1984), most notably with the Cincinnati Royals, Kansas City - Omaha Kings and Boston Celtics. In the 1972-1973 season Archibald led the NBA in scoring and assists becoming the only player to win the titles in both categories in the same season. A six-time NBA All-Star Archibald was named to the NBA's 50th Anniversary All-Time team and was inducted to the Naismith Basketball Hall of Fame in 1991.

Jonathan Southworth 'John' Ritter
September 17, 1948
September 11, 2003

Actor and comedian, best known for his role as Jack Tripper in Three's Company for which he won an Emmy and a Golden Globe Award in 1984. He appeared many films and television shows throughout his career and performed on Broadway in The Dinner Party (2000) at the Music Box Theatre. Ritter also received four Daytime Emmy Award nominations for his voice work on the children's television series Clifford The Big Red Dog.

Glenn Lewis Frey
November 6, 1948
January 18, 2016

Singer, songwriter and actor, best known as a founding member of the rock band the Eagles. Frey was the lead singer and frontman for the Eagles, roles he shared with fellow band member Don Henley with whom he wrote most of the Eagles' material. In 1980 Frey embarked on a successful solo career. As a member of the Eagles he won six Grammy Awards and five American Music Awards. The Eagles were inducted into the Rock and Roll Hall of Fame in 1998.

Clifford Allen 'Cliff' Harris
November 12, 1948

Former professional American Football safety who played for the Dallas Cowboys of the National Football League for ten seasons. He appeared in five Super Bowls (winning twice in Super Bowls VI and XII) and was selected to six consecutive Pro Bowls. To the Cowboys surprise Harris announced his retirement from football aged 31 to focus on his work within the oil business. In 2004 he was added to the Dallas Cowboys Ring of Honor.

Theodore Anthony 'Ted' Nugent
December 13, 1948

Musician and political activist who initially gained fame in 1963 as the lead guitarist of the Amboy Dukes. Nugent went solo in 1975 signing to Epic Records and releasing the multi-platinum albums; Ted Nugent (1975), Free-for-All (1976) and Cat Scratch Fever (1977). Nugent is noted for his conservative political views, is a board member of the National Rifle Association and a strong supporter of the Republican Party.

Samuel Leroy Jackson
December 21, 1948

Actor and film producer who achieved prominence and critical acclaim with films such as Jungle Fever (1991), Patriot Games (1992), Jurassic Park (1993), Pulp Fiction (1994), Django Unchained (2012) and The Hateful Eight (2015). He has provided his voice to many animated films, television series and video games, and altogether has appeared in over 100 films. Jackson is notably ranked as the highest all-time box office star grossing over $4,904.9 million.

Donna Summer - LaDonna Adrian Gaines
December 31, 1948
May 17, 2012

Singer, songwriter, painter and actress, who gained prominence during the disco era of the late 1970s. A five-time Grammy Award winner, she was the first artist to have three consecutive double albums reach No.1 on the U.S. Billboard 200 chart. Summer had a top 40 hit every year between 1975 and 1984 with 14 of those reaching the top ten. Reportedly selling over 140 million records worldwide she was inducted into the Rock and Roll Hall of Fame in 2013.

POPULAR MUSIC 1948

No.1	Dinah Shore	Buttons & Bows
No.2	Pee Wee Hunt	12th Street Rag
No.3	Nat King Cole	Nature Boy
No.4	Art Mooney	I'm Looking Over A Four Leaf Clover
No.5	Kay Kyser	The Woody Woodpecker Song
No.6	Peggy Lee	Mañana (Is Soon Enough For Me)
No.7	Bing Crosby	Now Is The Hour
No.8	Doris Day	It's Magic
No.9	Margaret Whiting	A Tree In The Meadow
No.10	Spike Jones	All I Want For Christmas Is My Two Front Teeth

Dinah Shore
Buttons & Bows

Label:
Columbia (D.B. 2446)

Written by:
Jay Livingston / Raymond Evans

Length:
2 mins 4 secs

Dinah Shore (born Frances Rose Shore; February 29, 1916 - February 24, 1994) was a singer, actress, television personality and the top-charting female vocalist during the Big Band era of the 1940s and 1950s. After failing singing auditions for Benny Goodman, Jimmy Dorsey and his brother Tommy Dorsey, Shore struck out on her own achieving huge solo success.

Pee Wee Hunt
12ᵗʰ Street Rag

Label:
Capitol Records (CL 13002)

Written by:
Euday Bowman / James Sumner

Length:
2 mins 46 secs

Pee Wee Hunt (born Walter Gerhardt Hunt; May 10, 1907 - June 22, 1979) was a jazz trombonist, vocalist and band leader. His 'Twelfth Street Rag' was a No.1 hit in September 1948 and sold over three million records.

3 Nat King Cole
Nature Boy

Label:	Written by:	Length:
Capitol Records (15054)	Eden Ahbez	2 mins 50 secs

Nathaniel Adams Coles (March 17, 1919 - February 15, 1965), known professionally as Nat King Cole, was a singer who first came to prominence as a leading jazz pianist. He was widely noted for his soft baritone voice performing in big band and jazz genres. Cole was one of the first African Americans to host a national television variety show, The Nat King Cole Show.

4 Art Mooney
I'm Looking Over A Four Leaf Clover

Label:	Written by:	Length:
MGM Records (10119)	Harry Woods / Mort Dixon	2 mins 26 secs

Arthur Joseph 'Art' Mooney (February 11, 1911 - September 9, 1993) was a singer and bandleader. His biggest hits were I'm Looking Over a Four Leaf Clover and Baby Face in 1948, and Nuttin' For Christmas, with Barry Gordon, in 1955. His fourth million selling song, Honey Babe, was used in the film Battle Cry (1955).

⑤ Kay Kyser
The Woody Woodpecker Song

Label:	Written by:	Length:
V Disc (849)	George Tibbles / Ramey Idriss	3 mins 9 secs

James Kern 'Kay' Kyser (June 18, 1905 - July 23, 1985) was an American bandleader and radio personality of the 1930s and 1940s. The Woody Wood Pecker Song (sung by Gloria Wood) received an Oscar nomination for the best song in 1949 and remained at No.1 in the charts for six weeks.

⑥ Peggy Lee
Mañana (Is Soon Enough For Me)

Label:	Written by:	Length:
Capitol Records (15022)	Dave Barbour / Peggy Lee	2 mins 53 secs

Peggy Lee (born Norma Deloris Egstrom; May 26, 1920 - January 21, 2002) was a jazz and popular music singer, songwriter, composer and actress. In a career spanning six decades this recording of Mañana (backed by Dave Barbour's Orchestra) became her biggest charting hit. Lee was a recipient of three Grammy Awards and an inductee of the Songwriters Hall Of Fame (1999).

7   Bing Crosby
Now Is The Hour

Label:	Written by:	Length:
Decca (L 4541)	Scott / Stewart / Kaihan	3 mins 10 secs

Harry Lillis 'Bing' Crosby, Jr. (May 3, 1903 - October 14, 1977) was a singer and actor. Crosby's trademark warm bass-baritone voice made him the best-selling recording artist of the 20th century selling close to a billion records, tapes, compact discs and digital downloads worldwide.

8   Doris Day
It's Magic

Label:	Written by:	Length:
Columbia (38188)	Jule Styne / Sammy Cahn	3 mins 5 secs

Doris Day (born Doris Mary Ann Kappelhoff; April 3, 1922) is a retired actress and singer, and continuing animal welfare activist. It's Magic was introduced by Doris Day in her 1948 film debut, Romance on the High Seas.

Margaret Whiting
A Tree In The Meadow

Label:	Written by:	Length:
Capitol Records (15122)	Billy Reid	2 mins 47 secs

Margaret Eleanor Whiting (July 22, 1924 - January 10, 2011) was a singer of popular and country music whose career was at its peak during the 1940s and 1950s. Whiting's version of A Tree In The Meadow reached the Billboard charts on July 9, 1948 and lasted 23 weeks, peaking at and giving Whiting her first No.1 record.

Spike Jones (And His City Slickers)
All I Want For Christmas Is My Two Front Teeth

Label:	Written by:	Length:
RCA Victor (20-3177)	Donald Gardner	2 mins 21 secs

Lindley Armstrong 'Spike' Jones (December 14, 1911 - May 1, 1965) was a musician and bandleader specializing in satirical arrangements of popular songs. Ballads and classical works receiving the Jones treatment were punctuated with gunshots, whistles, cowbells and outlandish vocals. All I Want For Christmas Is My Two Front Teeth (with vocals by George Rock) was Jones' only No.1 record.

TOP FILMS 1948

1. The Red Shoes
2. The Three Musketeers
3. Red River
4. The Treasure Of The Sierra Madre
5. Easter Parade

OSCARS

Best Film: Hamlet

Best Director: John Huston
(The Treasure Of The Sierra Madre)
Best Actor: Laurence Olivier
(Hamlet)
Best Actress: Jane Wyman
(Johnny Belinda)
Best Supporting Actor: Walter Huston
(The Treasure Of The Sierra Madre)
Best Supporting Actress: Claire Trevor
(Key Largo)

THE RED SHOES

Directed by: Michael Powell & Emeric Pressburger - Runtime: 134 minutes

"Dance she did, and dance she must— between her two loves"

J. Arthur Rank Presents
a Production of The Archers

ANTON WALBROOK

MARIUS GORING

MOIRA SHEARER

Leonide Massine

Robert Helpmann

Albert Basserman

Esmond Knight

Ludmilla Tcherina

A Dancing, Singing, Swinging Love Tale

Colour by Technicolor

Written, Produced and Directed by MICHAEL POWELL and EMERIC PRESSBURGER
DISTRIBUTION BY THE J. ARTHUR RANK OVERSEAS FILM DISTRIBUTORS LTD.

Young ballerina Victoria Page is poised for superstardom but is torn between the man she loves and her pursuit to become a prima ballerina.

STARRING

Anton Walbrook
Born: November 19, 1896
Died: August 9, 1967

Character:
Boris Lermontov

Adolf Anton Wilhelm Wohlbrück was an Austrian actor who settled in the United Kingdom under the name Anton Walbrook. He was descended from ten generations of actors although his father broke with tradition and was a circus clown. Walbrook studied with the director Max Reinhardt and built up a career in Austrian theatre and cinema before going to Hollywood in 1936. His last film was I accuse! (1958).

Marius Goring, CBE
Born: May 23, 1912
Died: September 30, 1998

Character:
Julian Craster

An English stage and film actor who is most often remembered for the four films he made with Powell & Pressburger, particularly as Conductor 71 in A Matter Of Life And Death (1946). Goring was fluent in both French and German and regularly performed French and German roles. He was made a Fellow of the Royal Society of Literature in 1979 and appointed Commander of the Order of the British Empire (CBE) in 1991.

Moira Shearer
Born: January 17, 1926
Died: January 31, 2006

Character:
Victoria Page

An actress and internationally renowned ballet dancer who came to international attention for her first film role as Victoria Page in The Red Shoes. Although she went on to star in other films and worked as a dancer for many decades, she is primarily known for playing 'Vicky'. Shearer also wrote for The Daily Telegraph newspaper and gave talks on ballet worldwide.

TRIVIA

Goofs

Just before Julian Craster begins to play the piano for the first time for Lermontov the shadow of a boom mic can be seen moving into position, projected against the wall behind him.

When Vicky begins to dance with the newspaper character only the words 'Le Journal' are typed across his face. Partway through the dance his face is covered with newsprint.

Interesting Facts

Jack Cardiff deliberately manipulated camera speed during the Red Shoes ballet to create the effect of dancers almost hovering in mid-air at the peak of their jumps.

Interesting Facts

When Ludovic Kennedy saw Moira Shearer in this film he said that he knew instantly that she was going to be the girl he would marry. He actively sought her out and married her two years later in the Chapel Royal in London's Hampton Court Palace.

Casting the role of Vicky Page was a tough call for Michael Powell and Emeric Pressburger. Ideally they wanted a ballerina who could act and who also had to be ravishingly beautiful. They were thrilled when they discovered Moira Shearer, who was second to Margot Fonteyn at the famous Sadler's Wells Ballet, but she initially rebuffed them. It took them a year to persuade her to change her mind.

The Red Shoes was nominated for 5 Academy Awards winning two, Best Original Score and Best Art Direction.

A restored print has been made by Martin Scorsese's Film Foundation and the UCLA Film & Television Archive, after many years work. The restorers went right back to the original negatives, digitally repairing any scratches and misalignment. The restored print was shown at Cannes in 2009 to great acclaim.

Quote

Boris Lermontov: Why do you want to dance?
([Vicky thinks for a short while]
Victoria Page: Why do you want to live?
[Lermontov is surprised at the answer]
Boris Lermontov: Well I don't know exactly why, er, but I must.
Victoria Page: That's my answer too.

THE THREE MUSKETEERS

Directed by: George Sidney - Runtime: 125 minutes

D'Artagnan and his musketeer comrades, Athos, Porthos and Aramis, thwart the plans of Royal Prime Minister Richelieu to usurp the King's power.

STARRING

Lana Turner
Born: February 8, 1921
Died: June 29, 1995

Character:
Lady de Winter

Film and television actress who was discovered in 1937 and signed by Metro-Goldwyn-Mayer aged just 16. Turner first attracted attention in They Won't Forget (1937). During the early 1940s she established herself as a leading actress and her popularity continued during the 1950s with films such as Peyton Place (1957) for which she was nominated for an Academy Award for Best Actress.

Gene Kelly
Born: August 23, 1912
Died: February 2, 1996

Character:
D'Artagnan

Dancer, actor, singer, film director, producer and choreographer. He is best known today for his performances in films such as An American In Paris (1951), Anchors Aweigh (1945) and Singin' In The Rain (1952). Kelly received an Academy Honorary Award in 1952 for his career achievements and in 1999 the American Film Institute put him at 15th in their Greatest Male Stars of Classic Hollywood cinema list.

June Allyson
Born: October 7, 1917
Died: July 8, 2006

Character:
Constance

Stage, film and television actress, dancer, and singer, born Eleanor Geisman. She began her career as a dancer in short subject films in 1937 and in 1938 on Broadway. She signed with MGM in 1943 and rose to fame the following year in the musical Two Girls and a Sailor (1944). In 1951 she won the Golden Globe Award for Best Actress for her performance in the romantic comedy film Too Young to Kiss.

TRIVIA

Goofs

During the first sword fight scene Gascon splashes water out of a bird bath into his opponent's face. After the fight the musketeers walk away laughing and the camera overhead shot reveals that the bird bath is completely dry.

Near the end of the movie D'Artagnan removes and drops his hat as he leaps into the water from the castle parapet. Seconds later he is riding at full gallop with his hat on.

The storyline for the film takes place in 1625 yet shows King Louis XIII as an old man. In reality Louis (1601 to 1643) would have only been 24 years old at the time.

Interesting Facts Lana Turner originally accepted a studio suspension in preference to playing Lady de Winter because she considered her a secondary character.

Thirty-five year old Gene Kelly's character D'Artagnan was supposed to be nineteen at the beginning of the film.

Lana Turner was ordered to lose weight before filming began in what would be her first appearance in a color feature film.

Fearing pressure from church groups MGM had the script refer to Richelieu as Prime Minister rather than Cardinal. Almost all traces of him being a cardinal or a man of the church were removed.

Quotes **Constance Bonacieux:** Oh monsieur! Monsieur, you come from the heavens.
D'Artagnan: No mademoiselle, just from upstairs.

Athos: To die among friends. Can a man ask more? Can the world offer less? Who wants to live 'till the last bottle is empty? It's all-for one, d'Artagnan, and one for all.

RED RIVER

Directed by: Howard Hawks & Arthur Rosson - Runtime: 92 minutes

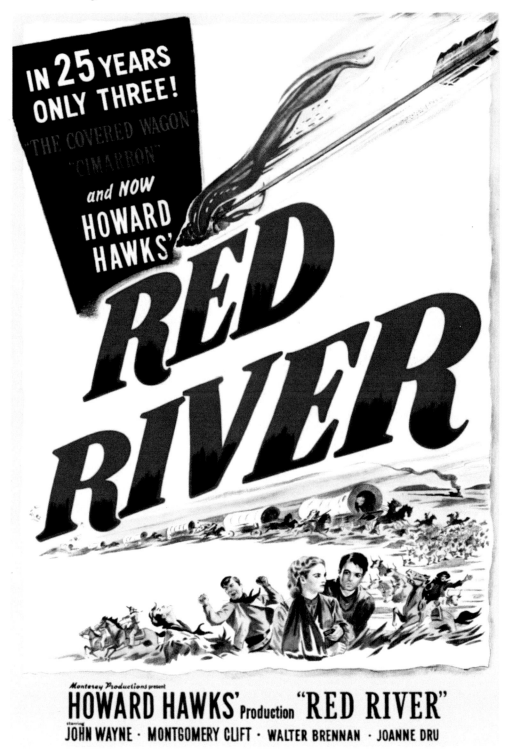

Tom Dunson leads a cattle drive to its destination 1,000 miles away in Missouri but his tyrannical behavior along the way causes a mutiny, led by his adopted son Matt Garth.

STARRING

John Wayne
Born: May 26, 1907
Died: June 11, 1979

Character:
Thomas Dunson

Actor, director and producer who was born Marion Robert Morrison. Nicknamed Duke, his career took off in 1939 with John Ford's Stagecoach making him an instant star. Wayne went on to star in a further 141 pictures and was nominated for an Academy Award on three occasions, winning once for Best Actor in True Grit (1969). He was posthumously awarded the Presidential Medal of Freedom on June 9, 1980.

Montgomery Clift
Born: October 17, 1920
Died: July 23, 1966

Character:
Matt Garth

Film and stage actor who is best remembered for his roles in Red River (1948), The Heiress (1949), A Place in the Sun (1951), I Confess (1952), From Here to Eternity (1953) and Judgment at Nuremberg (1961). Along with Marlon Brando and James Dean, Clift was one of the original method actors in Hollywood. He received four Academy Award nominations during his career, three for Best Actor and one for Best Supporting Actor.

Joanne Dru
Born: January 31, 1922
Died: September 10, 1996

Character:
Tess Millay

Film and television actress best known for films such as Red River, All the King's Men (1949) and The Pride of St. Louis (1952). Her film career petered out by the end of the 1950s but she continued working frequently in television, most notably as Babs Wooten on the 1960-61 sitcom Guestward, Ho!. For her contribution to the television industry Dru was awarded a star on the Hollywood Walk of Fame on February 8, 1960.

TRIVIA

Goofs

The film is set in 1865 yet several 1873 Colt Single-Action Army Revolvers and 1892 Winchesters are seen throughout the film.

During the cattle stampede Dunson, Matt and the other cowboys saddle up and try to turn the herd. Process shots of each cowboy are inserted in the scene. Every cowboy is riding the same dummy horse and saddle with a very large Mexican saddlehorn.

At the end of the film when Dunson finally confronts Matt and after knocking Matt down twice, Matt punches back knocking Dunson's hat off. The very next punch from Matt knocks Dunson's hat off again.

CONTINUED

Interesting Facts   After seeing John Wayne's performance in Red River, directed by rival director Howard Hawks, John Ford is quoted as saying, 'I never knew the big son of a bitch could act.' This led to Ford casting Wayne in more complex roles in films such as She Wore a Yellow Ribbon (1949) and The Searchers (1956).

Texas Longhorn cattle had been virtually extinct for about 50 years when this film was made and only a few dozen animals were available. In the herd scenes most of the cattle are Hereford crosses with the precious Longhorns being prominently placed during crucial scenes.

In an interview with Life Magazine, John Wayne described Montgomery Clift as 'an arrogant little bastard'.

The Treasure Of The Sierra Madre

Directed by: John Huston - Runtime: 126 minutes

Fred C. Dobbs and Bob Curtin, two Americans searching for work in Mexico, convince an old prospector to help them mine for gold in the Sierra Madre Mountains.

STARRING

Humphrey Bogart
Born: December 25, 1899
Died: January 14, 1957

Character:
Fred C. Dobbs

Screen and stage actor whose performances in films such as The Maltese Falcon (1941), Casablanca (1942) and The Big Sleep (1946) earned him status as a cultural icon. During a 30 year film career he appeared in more than 75 films, receiving three Oscar nominations for Best Actor and winning one for The African Queen (1951). In 1999 the American Film Institute ranked Bogart as the greatest male star of Classic American cinema.

Walter Huston
Born: April 5, 1883
Died: April 7, 1950

Character:
Howard

A Canadian-born American actor and singer. Huston won the Academy Award for Best Supporting Actor for his role in The Treasure Of The Sierra Madre, directed by his son John Huston (who won an Oscar for Best Director thus making them the first father and son to win at the same ceremony). He is a member of the American Theatre Hall of Fame and in 1960 was honored with a star on the Hollywood Walk of Fame.

Tim Holt
Born: February 5, 1919
Died: February 15, 1973

Character:
Bob Curtin

Film actor best known for his youthful leading roles in dozens of westerns along with his co-starring role in The Treasure Of The Sierra Madre. Holt was a World War II decorated combat veteran flying in the Pacific with the U.S. Army Air Forces as a B-29 bombardier. He was wounded over Tokyo on the last day of the war for which he received a Purple Heart. He was also a recipient of the Distinguished Flying Cross.

TRIVIA

Goofs

Although set in Mexico in the 1920s many of the cars on the street in the Tampico scenes are from the 1930s and 1940s.

As Dobbs is looking around trying to find Curtin's body, so that he can bury it, he runs into some bushes. As the camera pans round to follow him you can plainly see where the set ends (a large water tank and a hose are visible to the left).

Interesting Facts

A doctor assigned to the film in Mexico had to attend to John Huston one night when he had an adverse reaction to marijuana (having smoked it for the first time with his father). He never touched the stuff again.

CONTINUED

Interesting Facts

In his Oscar acceptance speech, Walter Huston said, 'Many many years ago I brought up a boy and I said to him, Son, if you ever become a writer try to write a good part for your old man sometime. Well, by cracky, that's what he did!'

Humphrey Bogart started losing his hair in 1947 partly due to the hormone shots he was taking to improve his chances of having a child with wife Lauren Bacall (although his excessive drinking and lack of vitamin B were probably also factors in his hair loss). He was completely bald by the time he arrived in Mexico for filming. Once on location Bogart started taking vitamin B shots and some of his hair grew back but not enough and he was forced to sport a wig throughout the entire shoot.

John Huston played one of his infamous practical jokes on Bruce Bennett in the campfire scene in which he eats a plate of stew. Bennett knew that his character was supposed to be starving so he wolfed down the food as quickly as possible. Huston then demanded another take and then another. In both extra takes the rapidly filling-up Bennett again had to eat a large plate of stew. Unbeknownst to him Huston had been happy with the first take and the cameras weren't even rolling for the second and the third, he just wanted to see how much food Bennett could eat before he became too stuffed. As soon as the joke was revealed Huston added insult to injury by calling for a lunch break.

Quotes

Bob Curtin: Wouldn't it be better the way things are to separate tomorrow or even tonight?
Fred C. Dobbs: That would suit you fine wouldn't it?
Bob Curtin: Why me more than you?
Fred C. Dobbs: So you could fall on me from behind, sneak up and shoot me in the back.
Bob Curtin: All right I'll go first.
Fred C. Dobbs: And wait for me on the trail to ambush me?

Bob Curtin: Remember what you said back in Tampico about having to carry that old man on our backs?
Fred C. Dobbs: That was when I took him for an ordinary human being, not part goat.

Easter Parade

Directed by: Charles Walters - Runtime: 107 minutes

A nightclub performer hires a naive chorus girl to become his new dance partner all to make his former partner jealous and to prove he can make any partner a star.

STARRING

Judy Garland
Born: June 10, 1922
Died: June 22, 1969

Character:
Hannah Brown

Singer and actress who began performing in vaudeville with her two older sisters and was signed to Metro-Goldwyn-Mayer as a teenager. Born Frances Ethel Gumm, she made more than two dozen films with MGM including nine with Mickey Rooney. Garland's most famous role was as Dorothy in The Wizard of Oz (1939). Aged 39 she became the youngest and first female recipient of the Cecil B. DeMille Award.

Fred Astaire
Born: May 10, 1899
Died: June 22, 1987

Character:
Don Hewes

Born Frederick Austerlitz, Astaire was an American dancer, choreographer, singer, musician and actor. His stage and subsequent film and television careers spanned a total of 76 years during which he made 31 musical films and several award-winning television specials. He is best known as the dancing partner and on-screen romantic interest of Ginger Rogers.

Peter Lawford
Born: September 7, 1923
Died: December 24, 1984

Character:
Jonathan Harrow III

British actor who lived in the U.S. throughout his adult life. His first major film role was in A Yank At Eton (1942), wherein he played a snobbish bully opposite Mickey Rooney. The film was a smash hit and his performance was widely praised. Lawford was a member of the 'Rat Pack' and brother-in-law to President John F. Kennedy. In later years he was noted more for his off-screen activities as a celebrity than for his acting.

TRIVIA

Goofs

During 'Steppin Out With My Baby', Hewes twirls a girl and her skirt floats up and revealed a black underskirt. However when twirled again she has a bright yellow underskirt.

When a police officer writes Jonathan (Peter Lawford) a ticket for parking beside a fire hydrant and hands over the ticket, he bumps the hydrant causing it to wobble.

While Hannah sings, 'It Only Happens When I Dance With You', she's supposed to be accompanying herself on the piano but her hands never reach the low notes that we hear.

CONTINUED

Interesting Facts   Gene Kelly was originally scheduled to play Don Hewes but he broke his ankle when he stamped his foot in anger after losing a volleyball game. It was at his suggestion that he be replaced by Fred Astaire.

Although she had been a star for years Judy Garland had never met Astaire before and was afraid to speak to him until they were properly introduced.

This film saw the debut of Jules Munshin. He plays the comic waiter who gives very entertaining descriptions of the menu items. A year later he would play one of the three sailors on leave in New York City in the film On The Town (1949) with Gene Kelly and Frank Sinatra.

Ann Miller had to perform her biggest numbers in the film in a back brace. In an interview with Robert Osborne she revealed that she had been thrown down the stairs by her then husband Reese Milner. She was also pregnant at the time and was in a lot of pain.

The song Easter Parade, which inspired the movie, was first sung in Irving Berlin's 1933 Broadway revue As Thousands Cheer, by Marilyn Miller and Clifton Webb. It was inspired by the annual event in New York City where people stroll down Fifth Avenue displaying their new hats (many of them often quite outrageous) and their Easter finery. The song also appeared in the Irving Berlin movie Holiday Inn (1942).

Quotes   **Don Hewes:** A girl dancer has to be exotic; she has to be a peach.
Hannah Brown: I suppose I'm a lemon!

Hannah Brown: *[her eyes are closed]* What colour are my eyes?
Don Hewes: *[kissing her, causing her to open her eyes in surprise]* Brown.

Don Hewes: Miss Brown, what idiot ever told you you were a dancer?
Hannah Brown: You did.

SPORTING WINNERS

LOU BOUDREAU - BASEBALL

ASSOCIATED PRESS - MALE ATHLETE OF THE YEAR

Louis 'Lou' Boudreau
Born: July 17, 1917 in Harvey, Illinois
Died: August 10, 2001 in Olympia Fields, Illinois

Lou Boudreau was a professional baseball player and manager who played in Major League Baseball (MLB) for 15 seasons, primarily as a shortstop on the Cleveland Indians. He also managed four teams for 15 seasons including 10 seasons as a player-manager. Boudreau was an All-Star for seven seasons and in 1948 he won the American League's Most Valuable Player Award with the Cleveland Indians whilst also managing them to the World Series title. In 1970 Boudreau was elected to the National Baseball Hall of Fame.

Career Summary:

Player	Years		Manager	Year
Cleveland Indians	1938-1950		Cleveland Indians	1942-1950
Boston Red Sox	1951-1952		Boston Red Sox	1952-1954
			Kansas City Athletics	1955-1957
			Chicago Cubs	1960

All Star 1940-1944, 1947, 1948 / American League Batting Champion 1944
World Series Champion 1948 / American League Most Valued Player 1948

FANNY BLANKERS-KOEN - TRACK & FIELD
ASSOCIATED PRESS - FEMALE ATHLETE OF THE YEAR

Francina 'Fanny' Elsje Blankers-Koen
Born: April 26, 1918 in Lage Vuursche, Netherlands
Died: January 25, 2004 in Hoofddorp, Netherlands

Fanny Blankers-Koen was a Dutch athlete best known for winning four gold medals at the 1948 Summer Olympics in London. She accomplished this as a 30-year-old mother of two during a time when many disregarded women's athletics. Her background and performances earned her the nickname The Flying Housewife and she was the most successful athlete at the 1948 Summer Olympics.

Medals:

Event	100m	200m	80m Hurdles	4x100m Relay
1938 Euro Championships - Vienna	Bronze	Bronze	-	-
1946 Euro Championships - Oslo	-	-	Gold	Gold
1948 Olympics - London	Gold	Gold	Gold	Gold
1950 Euro Championships - Brussels	Gold	Gold	Gold	Silver

Apart from her four Olympic titles, five European titles and 58 Dutch championships, Blankers-Koen also set or tied 12 world records - the last was in the pentathlon in 1951 aged 33. She retired from athletics in 1955 after which she became captain of the Dutch female track and field team. In 1999 she was voted 'Female Athlete Of The Century' by the International Association of Athletics Federations (IAAF). Her Olympic victories are credited with helping to eliminate the belief that age and motherhood were a barrier to success.

GOLF

THE MASTERS - CLAUDE HARMON

The Masters Tournament is the first of the majors to be played each year and unlike the other major championships it is played at the same location - Augusta National Golf Club, Georgia. This was the 12th Masters Tournament and was held April 8-11. Harmon's four round score of 279 (9 under par) tied the record set by Ralph Guldahl in 1939. Primarily a club professional it was Harmon's only tour victory. The total prize fund was $10,000 with $2,500 going to the winner.

PGA CHAMPIONSHIP - BEN HOGAN

The 1948 and 30th PGA Championship was played May 19-25 at Norwood Hills Country Club in St. Louis, Missouri. Ben Hogan won the match play championship, 7 & 6 over Mike Turnesa in the final. It was Hogan's second and final PGA Championship victory and he became only the second of four players in history to win the U.S. Open and the PGA Championship in the same calendar year. The total prize fund was $17,700 and the winner's share was $3,500.

U.S. OPEN - BEN HOGAN

The U.S. Open Championship (established in 1895) was held June 10-12 at Riviera Country Club in Pacific Palisades, California, northwest of Los Angeles. Ben Hogan won the first of his four U.S. Open titles at the course and this was the third of Hogan's nine major titles. Hogan's 8-under-par set a U.S. Open record that stood until 2000 when it was broken by Tiger Woods with 12-under (broken again by Rory McIlroy in 2011 with 16-under). The total prize fund was $10,000 with Hogan taking home $2,000.

Claude Harmon

Ben Hogan

WORLD SERIES - CLEVELAND INDIANS

Cleveland Indians　　　4 - 2　　　**Boston Braves**

Total attendance: 358,362 - Average attendance: 59,727
Winning player's share: $6,772 - Losing player's share: $4,571

The World Series is the annual championship series of Major League Baseball. Played since 1903 between the American League (AL) champion team and the National League (NL) champion, it is determined through a best-of-seven playoff.

The 1948 World Series matched the Cleveland Indians against the Boston Braves. The Braves had won the National League pennant for the first time since the 'Miracle Braves' team of 1914, while the Indians had spoiled a chance for the only all-Boston World Series by winning a one-game playoff against the Boston Red Sox for the American League flag. The Indians won the Series in six games to capture their second championship and their first since 1920. It was the first World Series to be televised on a nationwide network and was announced by famed sportcasters Red Barber, Tom Hussey (in Boston) and Van Patrick (in Cleveland).

	Date	Score			Location	Time	Att.
1	Oct 6	**Braves**	1-0	Indians	Braves Field	1:42	40,135
2	Oct 7	Braves	1-4	**Indians**	Braves Field	2:14	39.633
3	Oct 8	**Indians**	2-0	Braves	Cleveland Stadium	1:36	70,306
4	Oct 9	**Indians**	2-1	Braves	Cleveland Stadium	1:31	81,897
5	Oct 10	Indians	5-11	**Braves**	Cleveland Stadium	2:39	86,288
6	Oct 11	Braves	3-4	**Indians**	Braves Field	2:16	40,103

Horse Racing

Triple Crown winner and 1948 Horse of the Year, Citation.

Citation (April 11, 1945 - August 8, 1970) was the eighth American Triple Crown winner and one of three major North American Thoroughbreds (along with Zenyatta and Cigar) to win at least 16 consecutive races in major stakes race competition. By the end of his three-year-old season in 1948 Citation had a record of 20 starts, 19 wins and $709,470, for a new single season record. For his performances he was named Horse of the Year gaining 161 of a possible 163 votes in the poll conducted by Turf and Sport Digest magazine. Later Citation would become the first horse in history to win one million dollars.

Kentucky Derby - Citation

The Kentucky Derby is held annually at Churchill Downs in Louisville, Kentucky on the first Saturday in May. The race is a Grade 1 stakes race for three-year-olds and is one and a quarter miles in length.

Preakness Stakes - Citation

The Preakness Stakes is held on the third Saturday in May each year at Pimlico Race Course in Baltimore, Maryland. It is a Grade 1 race run over a distance of 9.5 furlongs (1 3/16 miles) on dirt.

Belmont Stakes - Citation

The Belmont Stakes is Grade 1 race held every June at Belmont Park in Elmont, New York. It is 1.5 miles in length and open to three-year-old thoroughbreds. It takes place on a Saturday between June 5 and June 11.

FOOTBALL - NFL CHAMPIONSHIP

CHAMPIONSHIP GAME

Chicago Cardinals   0 - 7   **Philadelphia Eagles**

Played: December 19, 1948 at Shibe Park, Philadelphia, Pennsylvania.
Attendance: 36,309 (paid), 28,864 (actual)

The 1948 Championship Game was played in Philadelphia during a significant snowstorm and Bert Bell, the NFL commissioner, considered postponing the game, but the players for both teams wanted to play. The snow began at daybreak but by kickoff it was 4 inches deep with at a temperature of 27°F (−3°C). The paid attendance for the game was 36,309 but the actual turnout, because of the weather, was 28,864.

Division Results:

Eastern Division

Team	P	W	L	T	PCT	PF	PA
Philadelphia Eagles	**12**	**9**	**2**	**1**	**.818**	**376**	**156**
Washington Redskins	12	7	5	0	.583	291	287
New York Giants	12	4	8	0	.333	297	388
Pittsburgh Steelers	12	4	8	0	.333	200	243
Boston Yanks	12	3	9	0	.250	174	372

Western Division

Team	P	W	L	T	PCT	PF	PA
Chicago Cardinals	**12**	**11**	**1**	**0**	**.917**	**395**	**226**
Chicago Bears	12	10	2	0	.833	375	151
Los Angeles Rams	12	6	5	1	.545	327	269
Green Bay Packers	12	3	9	0	.250	154	290
Detroit Lions	12	2	10	0	.167	200	407

P= Games Played, W = Wins, L = Losses, T = Ties,
PCT= Winning Percentage, PF= Points For, PA = Points Against
Note: The NFL did not officially count tie games in the standings until 1972.

League Leaders

Statistic	Name	Team	Yards
Passing	Sammy Baugh	Washington Redskins	2599
Rushing	Steve Van Buren	Philadelphia Eagles	945
Receiving	Mal Kutner	Chicago Cardinals	943

Hockey: 1947-48 NHL Season

The 1947-48 NHL season was the 31st season of the National Hockey League with six teams each playing 60 games. The Toronto Maple Leafs were the Stanley Cup winners defeating the Detroit Red Wings 4-0.

Final Standings:

	Team	GP	W	L	T	GF	GA	Pts
1	**Toronto Maple Leafs**	**60**	**32**	**15**	**13**	**182**	**143**	**77**
2	Detroit Red Wings	60	30	18	12	187	148	72
3	Boston Bruins	60	23	24	13	167	168	59
4	New York Rangers	60	21	26	13	176	201	55
5	Montreal Canadiens	60	20	29	11	147	169	51
6	Chicago Black Hawks	60	20	34	6	195	225	46

Scoring Leaders:

	Player	Team	Goals	Assists	Points
1	**Elmer Lach**	**Montreal Canadiens**	**30**	**31**	**61**
2	Buddy O'Connor	New York Rangers	24	36	60
3	Doug Bentley	Chicago Black Hawks	20	37	57

Hart Trophy (Most Valuable Player): Bud O'Connor - New York Rangers
Vezina Trophy (Fewest Goals Allowed): Turk Broda - Toronto Maple Leafs

Stanley Cup

4 - 0

Toronto Maple Leafs   **Detroit Red Wings**

Series Summary:

	Date	Home Team	Result	Road Team
1	April 7	Detroit Red Wings	3-5	**Toronto Maple Leafs**
2	April 10	Detroit Red Wings	2-4	**Toronto Maple Leafs**
3	April 11	**Toronto Maple Leafs**	2-0	Detroit Red Wings
4	April 14	**Toronto Maple Leafs**	7-2	Detroit Red Wings

INDIANAPOLIS 500 - MAURI ROSE

Mauri Rose takes his 3rd Indy 500 win in a Lou Moore, Blue Crown Spark Plug Spl.

The 32nd International 500-Mile Sweepstakes Race was held at the Indianapolis Motor Speedway on Monday, May 31, 1948. For the second year in a row the Blue Crown Spark Plug teammates Mauri Rose and Bill Holland finished 1st and 2nd. Rose became the second driver to win the Indianapolis 500 in consecutive years and unlike the previous year's race no controversy surrounded the results. Coupled with his co-victory in 1941 Rose became the third three-time winner at Indianapolis.

Fourth place finisher Ted Horn completed a noteworthy record of nine consecutive races from 1936-1948 completing 1,799 out of a possible 1,800 laps. His nine consecutive finishes of 4th or better (however, with no victories) is the best such streak in Indy history. The only lap he missed in 1940 was due to being flagged for a rain shower.

BOSTON MARATHON GÉRARD CÔTÉ

The Boston Marathon is the oldest annual marathon in the world and dates back to 1897.

Race Result:

1.	**Gérard Côté (CAN)**	**2:31:02**
2.	Ted Vogel (USA)	2:31:46
3.	John A. Kelley (USA)	2:36:53

BASKETBALL - BAA FINALS

4 - 2

Baltimore Bullets   Philadelphia Warriors

The 1947-48 BAA season was the second season of the Basketball Association of America. The league consisted of 8 teams each playing a 48-game schedule. The 1948 BAA Playoffs ended with the Baltimore Bullets winning the BAA Championship by beating the Philadelphia Warriors 4 games to 2 in the BAA Finals.

LEAGUE SUMMARY

In the 1948-49 season the BAA and National Basketball League merged to create the National Basketball Association (NBA). Today the NBA recognizes the three BAA seasons as part of its own history.

Eastern Division:

	Team	GP	W	L	PCT	GB
1	**Philadelphia Warriors**	48	27	21	.563	-
2	New York Knicks	48	26	22	.542	1
3	Boston Celtics	48	20	28	.417	7
4	Providence Steamrollers	48	6	42	.125	21

Western Division:

	Team	GP	W	L	PCT	GB
1	**St. Louis Bombers**	48	29	19	.604	-
2	Baltimore Bullets	48	28	20	.583	1
3	Chicago Stags	48	28	20	.583	1
4	Washington Capitols	48	28	20	.583	1

Statistics Leaders:

	Player	Team	Stats
Points	Max Zaslofsky	Chicago Stags	1,007
Assists	Howie Dallmar	Philadelphia Warriors	120
FG%	Bob Feerick	Washington Capitols	.340
FT%	Bob Feerick	Washington Capitols	.788

Note: Prior to the 1969-70 season league leaders in points and assists were determined by totals rather than averages.

TENNIS - U.S. NATIONAL CHAMPIONSHIPS

Mens Singles Champion - Pancho Gonzales - United States
Ladies Singles Champion - Margaret Osborne duPont - United States

The 1948 U.S. National Championships (now known as the U.S. Open) took place on the outdoor grass courts at the West Side Tennis Club, Forest Hills in New York. The tournament ran from September 10-19 and was the 68th staging of the U.S. National Championships, and the fourth Grand Slam tennis event of the year.

Men's Singles Final:

Country	Player	Set 1	Set 2	Set 3
United States	Pancho Gonzales	6	6	14
South Africa	Eric Sturgess	2	3	12

Women's Singles Final:

Country	Player	Set 1	Set 2	Set 3
United States	Margaret Osborne duPont	4	6	15
United States	Louise Brough	6	4	13

Men's Doubles Final:

Country	Players	Set 1	Set 2	Set 3	Set 4	Set 5
United States	Gardnar Mulloy / Bill Talbert	1	9	6	3	9
United States	Frank Parker / Ted Schroeder	6	7	3	6	7

Women's Doubles Final:

Country	Players	Set 1	Set 2	Set 3
United States	Louise Brough / Margaret Osborne duPont	6	8	6
United States	Patricia Todd / Doris Hart	4	10	1

Mixed Doubles Final:

Country	Players	Set 1	Set 2
United States	Louise Brough / Tom Brown	6	6
United States	Margaret Osborne duPont / Bill Talbert	4	4

1948 SUMMER OLYMPICS

The 1948 Summer Olympics, officially known as the Games of the XIV Olympiad, were held in London from July 29 to August 14. The Games had 4,104 athletes from 59 National Olympic Committees participating in a total of 136 events. These were the first Summer Olympics since 1936 due to WWII and had the highest number of nations represented at any Games to date (Germany and Japan were refused permission to participate and although the USSR was invited it chose not to send any athletes).

Medals Table:

Rank	Nation	Gold	Silver	Bronze	Total
1	**United States**	**38**	**27**	**19**	**84**
2	Sweden	16	11	17	44
3	France	10	6	13	29
4	Hungary	10	5	12	27
5	Italy	8	11	8	27
12	Great Britain & NI	3	14	6	23

One of the star performers at the Games was Dutch sprinter Fanny Blankers-Koen. Dubbed The Flying Housewife, the 30-year-old mother of two won four gold medals in athletics. In the decathlon, American Bob Mathias became the youngest male ever to win an Olympic gold medal at the age of 17.

U.S. Medals:

Sport	1	2	3	Sport	1	2	3
Athletics	12	5	10	Basketball	1	0	0
Swimming	8	6	1	Canoeing	1	2	0
Diving	4	4	2	Shooting	1	1	0
Weightlifting	4	3	1	Boxing	0	1	0
Wrestling	2	1	1	Modern Pentathlon	0	1	0
Sailing	2	1	1	Fencing	0	0	1
Rowing	2	0	1	Gymnastics	0	0	1
Equestrian	1	2	0	Medal Totals	38	27	19

THE COST OF LIVING

COMPARISON CHART

	1948	1948 Price Today (Including Inflation)	2017	Real Term % Change
House	$14,200	$143,534	$290,400	+102.3%
Annual Income	$1,650	$16,678	$54,920	+229.3%
Car	$1,950	$19,711	$32,994	+67.4%
Gallon of Gasoline	25¢	$2.53	$2.32	-8.3%
Gallon of Milk	31¢	$3.13	$4.04	+29.1%
DC Comic Book	10¢	$1.01	$3.99	+295%

IT'S BEEF THAT MAKES THIS NOODLE SOUP

YOU TASTE BEEF ALL THROUGH IT!

Campbell's
CONDENSED
BEEF NOODLE
SOUP

Have you tried this fast-growing favorite?

The taste of beef through and through —that's what you get in Campbell's Beef Noodle Soup. That's what has won it a welcome everywhere, though it's still one of Campbell's newer soups. Fine lean beef is slow-simmered to make a rich invigorating broth. Steeped in that good beef broth are golden egg noodles. And generously measured in are tender pieces of beef. Campbell's Beef Noodle is a soup to know in times like these—a main dish soup that puts the hearty taste of beef in many a lunch and supper.

Campbell's
BEEF NOODLE SOUP
LOOK FOR THE RED-AND-WHITE LABEL

It's good! It's new!
In favor fast-growing;
It's BEEF straight through—
A soup worth the knowing!

SHOPPING

Mrs Wright's White Bread Loaf (24oz)	18¢
Fresh Eggs (large mixed dozen)	57¢
Eagle Brand Milk (15oz can)	25¢
Carnation Milk (4 small cans)	25¢
Wisconsin Cheese (per lb)	59¢
Aged American Cheddar Cheese (per lb)	55¢
Sunshine Hi-Lo Crackers (1lb box)	27¢
American Beauty Flour (5lb bag)	53¢
Jane Parker Donuts (x12)	19¢
Bakers Bitter Chocolate Bar	30¢
M&M Candy Coated Chocolate (7oz pkg.)	25¢
Texas Oranges (8lb bag)	29¢
Golden Delicious Apples (per lb)	10¢
Lemons (2lb)	15¢
Watermelons (ice cold - per lb)	2¢
Whole Apricots In Heavy Syrup (#2½ can)	19¢
Cherries (#2 can)	33¢
Tomatoes (2x #2 cans)	25¢
Russet Potatoes No.1 (5lb)	33¢
Sno-White Cauliflower Heads (per lb)	15¢
Fresh Valley Spinach (per lb)	15¢
Pictsweet Peas (#2 can)	19¢
Bonners Country Sausage (per lb)	75¢
Franco American Spaghetti (x2)	29¢
Picnic Ham (per lb)	49¢
Steak Loin (per lb)	63¢
Calf Liver (per lb)	55¢
Full Dressed Hens (per lb)	45¢
Baltimore Oysters (per lb)	79¢
South Pacific Sardines (15oz can)	21¢
Star Kist Grated Tuna (6oz can)	43¢
Premium Sliced Bacon (per lb)	83¢
Campbell's Chicken Soup (2x regular cans)	31¢
Chow-Mein Noodles (#2 can)	24¢
Heinz Baby Food (3x cans)	23¢
Jell-Well Gelatins (2x assorted flavors)	13¢
Airway Coffee (per lb)	40¢
8 O'Clock Coffee (1lb bag)	40¢
Nectar Tea Bags (x48)	41¢
Texsun Gr'p'fruit Juice (3x #2 can)	25¢
Libbys Tomato Juice (2x #2 can)	25¢
Halo Shampoo	69¢
Gillette Shave Cream	29¢
Camey Soap (bar)	10¢
Kleenex (200 size box)	15¢
Rinso (large pkg.)	33¢
Smith Brothers Cough Drops	5¢
Listerine	69¢

For a BRIGHT start

MOTHER KNOWS BEST
—and more mothers buy Kellogg's Cereals for their children than any other brand! Choose from six grand

favorites in *Kellogg's Variety*. Corn, wheat, rice! Flakes, shreds, pops! Crisper 'cause they're fresher. So economical, too! No other assortment includes . . .

KELLOGG'S RICE KRISPIES
—the *only* cereal so crisp it snaps, crackles and pops in milk! So delicious . . . so nourishing . . . it's America's most popular ready-to-eat rice cereal. Buy it in the thrifty family size, too . . . Eat a Better Breakfast—start with Rice Krispies!

Mother Knows Kellogg's Best!

58

CLOTHES

Women's Clothing

Squirrel Locks Fur Coat	$175
J. M. Dyer Raincoats	$13.95 - $26.95
Handmacher Celanese Suit	$18.75
Blackburn Fashion Shop Summer Dresses	$10.95 - $19.95
Ann Foster Summer Blouses	$3.95 - $9.95
Wool Skirt	$5.95 - $11.95
Bra Suit & Pedal Pushers	$4.95
Printed Satin Robe	$8.95
Sears Honeylane Slip	$2.19
Rayon Panties	66¢
Rhythm Steps Black Patent Shoes	$12.95
Zombie Sandals	$1.49
Airmaid Nylon Hose	$1.35 - $2.50

Men's Clothing

Sports Coat	$10
Stetson 3X Beaver	$16.50
Horsehide Jacket	$10
Rockingham Premium Worsted Suit	$45
Dress Shirts	$1.88 - $2.88
Manhattan T-Shirt	$1 - $2.75
Hickok Matching Tie, Bar & Cuff Links	$5
P. Samuels Rayon Slacks	$8.50
Manhattan Striped Pyjamas	$5 - $6.50
McGregor Swim Shorts	$2.95 - $6
Jarman Shoes (most styles)	$11.95 - $13.95
Penny's Fine Handkerchiefs	39¢

SWEATERS

100% NYLON
feather-light, super-strong!

$2.89 $4.89 $3.79

The Christmas gift he'll remember for life—

...a Schwinn-Built bicycle!

When *your* young hopeful asks for a *Schwinn-Built* bike for Christmas you may be mighty sure he, or she, has the word on bicycles! For among youngsters—America's real "bike experts"—Schwinn rates a *four-to-one* favorite over any other make.

For over 50 years, Arnold, Schwinn & Company has been manufacturing bicycles that are unsurpassed for nifty looks and smooth riding, for long life and safety. Share the thrill of seeing that wonderful big Schwinn under *your* tree this Christmas. You can find your nearest Schwinn dealer in your Classified Telephone Directory listed under "bicycles."

Slick Riding!
The Schwinn Spring Fork gives a smooth, cloud-like ride.

Long Lasting!
Every Schwinn frame is electronically welded for life-time strength and wear.

Great Schwinn Extras!
Schwinn Cycelock, Built-in kick stand, Fore-Wheel brake, are but a few of them.

Amazing Guarantee!
Ask about the "Long As You Own It" guarantee. Comes with every Schwinn-Built bicycle.

Look for this famous seal before you buy a bike!

OF COURSE, SCHWINN-BUILT BIKES FOR GIRLS ARE SUPER-TERRIFIC, TOO! JUST AS SMOOTH AND STRONG AS THE BOYS!

4 TIMES AS MANY KIDS WANT A SCHWINN AS WANT ANY OTHER BIKE.

ARNOLD, SCHWINN & COMPANY
CHICAGO, ILLINOIS
America's Finest Bicycles

60

TOYS

Western Flyer Bicycle (boys or girls)	$39.95
Aluminum Tricycle	$9.95
Scooter	$1.25
Bing Crosby Junior Juke	$30.25
6-Room Happi-Time Dolls House	$3.84
13" Red Bass Drum With Cymbals	98¢
Sears 8-Piece Cowboy / Cowgirl Sets	$7.45
G-Man Machine Gun	$1.98
Little Doctors Medical Kit	$1.49
Metal Cash Register	$3.89
Mickey Mouse Wrist Watch	$6.95
Marx Electric Train Set	$15.45
'New York Central' Wind Up Train	$3.89
All Metal Dump Truck	79¢
Union Brand Roller Skates	$3.45

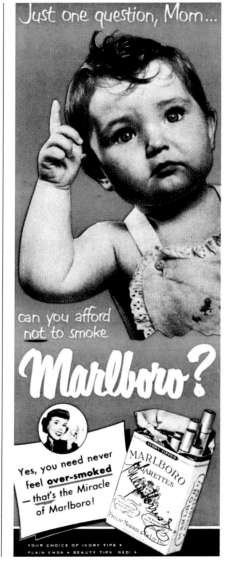

Belmont RADIO
AM-FM
and
TELEVISION
for
1948

Model 22AX22 • DELUXE TELEVISION CONSOLE

● A truly fine television console, bringing the whole world of sports, news events and drama to the home—and housed in an attractive mahogany cabinet of dignified harmonious design. Super-sized picture image of 55 square inches insures easy vision for the entire family group. Covers both television bands—channels 1 through 13. Powerful 20-tube chassis plus two rectifier tubes. Noise-free FM television sound. Large 10" cathode-ray viewing tube gives splendid definition and a clear concise picture. 110-volt AC operation only. Finished in mahogany, hand rubbed to bring out the beauty of the wood.

Model 22A21
TABLE MODEL TELEVISION RECEIVER

● This superb table model Television receiver provides the latest developments in Television engineering—brings the joy and pleasure of viewing on-the-spot events to the home. Model 22A21 is a 20-tube (plus two rectifier tubes) Television receiver covering the complete Television band, channels 1 through 13. Noise-free FM television sound. Provides large 7-inch electrostatically deflected picture tube giving exceptionally fine definition and a brilliant, easy-to-view picture. 110-volt AC operation only. Handsome mahogany cabinet. Size: 14½" x 21" x 15".

OTHER ITEMS

Chevrolet Stylemaster 2 Door Sport Coupe	$1323
Wizard Deluxe Car Battery	$10.95
Tires – Firestone Guaranteed New Treads	$7.35
Firestone 3.6 H.P. Single Cylinder Outboard Motor	$89.95
3 Piece Walnut Veneer Bedroom Suite	$148.88
Chrome Plated 5-Piece Dinette Set (porcelain top)	$59.95
Compact Kerogas Oil Range	$79.95
Deepfreeze Deluxe C10 Freezer - 10 Cubic Feet	$449.50
Zenith 'Georgian' FM-AM Radio Phonograph	$239.95
General Electric Sandwich Grill Waffle Iron	$11.95
Camfield Pop-Up Toaster	$19.95
Adjust-O-Matic Lightweight 1,000W Iron	$11.95
Sunbeam Shavemaster Electric Razor	$23.50
Luminous Dial Alarm Clock	$4.95
Wizard Radiant Gas Heater	$14.95
Twist Weave Carpet (per square yard)	$10
Penny's 4lb 72" x 90" Wool Blanket	$8.90
6-Piece Ladies Dresser Set	$9.90
La Zenda Cigars (box of 50)	$2.59
Carton Of Cigarettes (all brands)	$1.61
Yellow Bowl Pipe	$1
Fresh Green Northwestern Fir Christmas Tree (7-8ft.)	$1.29
Pear Tree (2-3ft)	89¢
Quality House Broom	65¢

U.S. COINS

Official Circulated U.S. Coins		Years Produced
Half-Cent	½¢	1792 - 1857
Cent (Penny)	1¢	1793 - Present
2-Cent	2¢	1864 - 1873
3-Cent	3¢	1851 - 1889
Half-Dime	5¢	1792 - 1873
Five Cent Nickel	5¢	1866 - Present
Dime	10¢	1792 - Present
20-Cent	20¢	1875 - 1878
Quarter	25¢	1796 - Present
Half Dollar	50¢	1794 - Present
Dollar Coin	$1	1794 - Present
Quarter Eagle	$2.50	1792 - 1929
Three-Dollar Piece	$3	1854 - 1889
Four-Dollar Piece	$4	1879 - 1880
Half Eagle	$5	1795 – 1929
Commemorative Half Eagle	$5	1980 - Present
Silver Eagle	$1	1986 - Present
Gold Eagle	$5	1986 - Present
Platinum Eagle	$10 - $100	1997 - Present
Double Eagle (Gold)	$20	1849 - 1933
Half Union	$50	1915

STAR SPANGLED NEW!

Hub caps at extra cost when available

Excitingly MODERN!
Strikingly DIFFERENT!

☆ **2 NEW BIG JOBS!**

Biggest Ford Trucks ever built! 145 H.P. engine! Up to 21,500 lbs. G.V.W.! Up to 10.00-20 tires!

☆ **NEW MILLION DOLLAR TRUCK CAB!**

With living room comfort! Biggest contribution to driver comfort in 20 years! New 3-way air control. New coach-type seats. New picture-window visibility! New Level Action cab suspension!

☆ **3 NEW TRUCK ENGINES!**

A new Six, two new V-8's! Most modern engine line in the truck field! Up to 145 H.P.! High turbulence combustion chambers! New Loadomatic ignition! 4-ring pistons!

☆ **OVER 139 NEW MODELS!**

Widest job coverage in Ford Truck history! Cab-Over-Engine and conventional chassis! Panel, Pickup, Express, Stake and Platform bodies! G.V.W. ratings 4,700 lbs. up to 21,500 lbs.

Listen to the Ford Theater over NBC stations Sunday afternoons, 5:00 to 6:00 p. m., E. S. T.

Hottest truck line in history . . . from the Leader in Trucks Built and Trucks in Use!

Our trucks are red-hot! That's because they're brand new! Ford *Bonus Built* Trucks for '48 are brand new in every important way but one!

Big exception is truck-building know-how! That isn't new with us! We've been building trucks for over 30 years! We've built more trucks and picked up more truck know-how than anyone else!

From a combination of the NEW in truck engineering and the KNOW-HOW of truck experience, you get new thrift! . . . new performance! . . . new reliability!

In Ford Trucks you get *Bonus Built* construction, the extra strength that pays off two ways. First, Ford *Bonus Built* Trucks are not limited to just one job, but are good all-around workers in a wide range of jobs. Second, Ford Trucks last longer. Life insurance experts *certify* proof that Ford Trucks last up to 19.6% longer!

Drop in on your Ford Dealer to size-up the new engines . . . new cabs . . . new BIG JOBS . . . over 139 new models in the biggest Ford Truck line in history!

*BONUS: *"Something given in addition to what is usual or strictly due."* — Webster's Dictionary

FORD 1948 *Bonus* Built* TRUCKS 1958

BUILT STRONGER TO LAST LONGER

Made in the USA
Monee, IL
05 December 2024

72582018R00040